Wartime Christmas

Wartime Christmas

BRITISH CELEBRATIONS DURING TWO WORLD WARS

Anthony Richards

Published by IWM, Lambeth Road, London SE1 6HZ
iwm.org.uk

ISBN 978-1-912423-23-1

A catalogue record for this book is available from the British Library

Printed and bound in the UK by Gomer Press
Colour reproduction by Zebra

All images © IWM unless otherwise stated
Front cover: Art.IWM PST 15609 (detail)
Back cover: Art. IWM PST 15124 (detail)

CONTENTS

INTRODUCTION

Christmas is a time for tradition. We exchange gifts, share meals together, and make a special effort to look out for those less fortunate than ourselves. We attach great importance to making sure that we enjoy ourselves as much as possible, just for that brief day or two at the end of each year.

For those living through the First World War (1914–1918) and Second World War (1939–1945), however, celebrating Christmas could prove very challenging indeed. Both conflicts were characterised by shortages of food and other resources; forced separation from loved ones; and above all the difficulty of reconciling a celebration of peace within the context of waging bloody war. While each world war was quite different in its own way, we will see that many of the characteristics of a wartime Christmas were shared across both eras. Readers of this book might spot a certain bias towards the Second World War, as that period suffered more dramatically from the shortages and extensive separation that most affected Christmas celebrations for ordinary people.

Putting the influence of wartime to one side, the kind of Christmas which was celebrated during the first half of the twentieth century did not differ markedly from the way in which people enjoy the festive season today. While we may point to the ever-greater commercialism attached to the modern version of the holiday, a strong sense of continuity can still be detected between today's Christmases and those enjoyed over a century ago.

CHRISTMAS CARD
THE CARD IS FREE
TO PURCHASERS OF
6ᴰ 2/6 & 5/- SAVINGS STAMPS

3% DEFENCE BONDS
FOR THOSE WHO WANT TO GIVE
THE LITTLE MORE
IN UNITS OF £5

GIFT TOKENS
SAVINGS CERTIFICATES
ARE EASY TO GIVE
THE 'TOKEN' WAY

Christmas Day has traditionally been celebrated both religiously and culturally as a public holiday. Indeed, our modern Christmas can be regarded as a modified version of ancient winter festivals practised since Roman times. Held around the Winter Solstice, towards the end of December, the Roman celebration of Saturnalia was characterised by drinking and feasting, dancing and singing and the exchange of presents. The normal order of things in society was deliberately reversed, with slaves being served by their masters, cross-dressing actively encouraged (an early form of today's pantomime) and children elevated to the highest importance. Over subsequent centuries many other faiths added to the celebration's mix, with Scandinavian traditions emphasising the importance of light in banishing the midwinter darkness, and Paganism adding elements such as evergreen trees and the yule log. When the early Christian faith began to celebrate the birth of Jesus, it therefore made sense for them to take over these existing traditions, adapting them to their own form of worship rather than abolishing them completely.

One aspect of Christmas which becomes particularly evident during war is the holiday's importance in creating social happiness.

Ready for Christmas: the Canteen under St Martin's-in-the-fields by Edmond Xavier Kapp, 1941.

A Second World War poster used to promote the importance of war savings. War savings certificates were first introduced in 1916 as a means to raise money for the nation while rewarding the investor with interest after a set period. By the Second World War they were an essential part of funding the conflict.

PAGE 6
This Ministry of Information photograph was taken as part of a series promoting the YMCA's charitable 'Gifts to Home League'. This scheme allowed troops serving overseas to choose birthday or Christmas gifts for their families back home. Here, the Devereux family from Pinner in Middlesex are shown opening their gifts in December 1944.

The earliest Roman festivals were a reward to its citizenry for obedience to the hierarchy, as well as an affirmation of the empire's prosperity. This annual return to a strong tradition centred on happiness was never more important than during a period of war, in which communities could be reminded that the privations and restrictions they were suffering throughout the rest of the year were worthwhile burdens. This idea of Christmas being a brief return to normality was a logical choice by people worn down by conflict. Sometimes it was a deliberate aspect of wartime propaganda, seized upon by governments and leaders to keep their populace's war effort on track.

But more than anything else, people adopted Christmas as a means to celebrate normality during the chaos of war. The experience was often a shared one, with friends and enemies largely celebrating the same holiday; sometimes for different reasons, but ultimately in an attempt to find peace and normality during a time of uncertainty in their lives. For this reason, and indeed throughout both world wars, people made every effort to celebrate the season in the best way they possibly could.

⌃

This Second World War advertisement, issued by the National Savings Committee, encourages the purchase of war savings certificates by employing the popular festive character of Father Christmas.

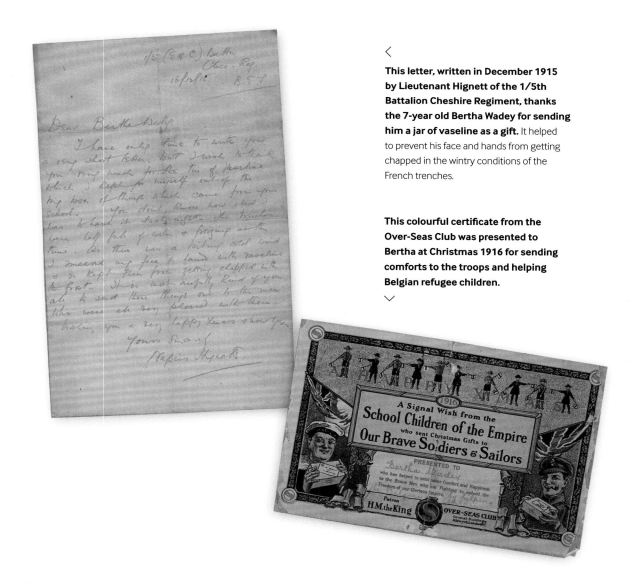

<

This letter, written in December 1915 by Lieutenant Hignett of the 1/5th Battalion Cheshire Regiment, thanks the 7-year old Bertha Wadey for sending him a jar of vaseline as a gift. It helped to prevent his face and hands from getting chapped in the wintry conditions of the French trenches.

This colourful certificate from the Over-Seas Club was presented to Bertha at Christmas 1916 for sending comforts to the troops and helping Belgian refugee children.

∨

Ceasefire or Business as Usual?

By Christmas 1914, the British Expeditionary Force (BEF) had entrenched itself on the Western Front of France and Belgium. The German advance that began in August that year had been halted for the moment, and as the winter stalemate set in, combatants of both sides would rethink their strategies and wait until the spring to embark on new campaigns. Until then it was largely a matter of sitting tight and defending their positions. Those commentators who had cheerfully predicted that the war would be short lived and 'over by Christmas' became resigned to the fact that it would clearly carry on well into 1915 and potentially for many more years to come. But, in a moment that surprised everybody, the soldiers themselves would seize a brief opportunity for peace during their first wartime Christmas.

PREVIOUS PAGE
British troops eating their Christmas dinner in a shell hole at Beaumont Hamel, France, 25 December 1916.

A photographic souvenir of the 1914 Christmas Truce. Shown here are British troops from the Northumberland Hussars fraternising with two German officers.

L

THE CHRISTMAS TRUCE

In the days leading up to 25 December, short truces were held to collect dead and wounded from the barren No Man's Land between the trenches. These were only brief episodes, however, with Christmas Eve bringing a greater surprise. In certain sectors of the line the festive spirit affected both armies as they began to sing Christmas carols and called out festive greetings to one another. Some soldiers even began a cautious fraternisation between the trenches, chatting and exchanging cigarettes and food with their enemy. More prolonged socialising took place on Christmas Day itself, as 2nd Lieutenant Willy Spencer recalled in a letter sent home a few days later.

There was no firing, so by degrees each side began gradually showing more of themselves, and then two of their men came halfway and called for an officer. I went out and found that they were willing to have an armistice for four hours, and to carry our dead men back halfway for us to bury. This I arranged and then — can you imagine it? — both sides came out, met in the middle, shook hands, wished each other compliments of the season, and had a chat. A strange sight between two hostile lines.

It was not just the British who participated, as similar stories emerged from those parts of the front manned by French and Belgian troops too. But such fraternisation was temporary and occurred only in certain sectors. As quickly as it began, the moment was over and within days the normal fighting had resumed.

Soldiers from the 2nd Battalion Gordon Highlanders photographed with German troops in the Rue de Quesnes sector of the Western Front, Christmas Day 1914.

To understand the 'Christmas Truce' of 1914 we should remember that it occurred very early on in the First World War. Initiatives for some kind of armistice had already been circulating in the run up to Christmas that year. An 'Open Christmas Letter' asking for peace and addressed to the women of Germany and Austria was signed by over a hundred British suffragettes, while Pope Benedict had publically called for an official truce. Christmas in 1914 would have felt like an odd situation, with many wondering why the conflict had not already seen a swift resolution. Soldiers from both sides had a duty to fight, but not necessarily to hate each other. With neither side not yet firmly committed to the urgent necessity for victory, the combatants' personal thoughts were just as likely to be infected by the benevolent atmosphere of Christmas rather than any earnestness to kill.

This poster, produced for the Scottish War Savings Committee in 1918, links the purchase of war savings certificates to the act of lighting a Christmas candle.

> *The End of the Cuxhaven Raid, Christmas Day, 1914* by R Pearson.

A DAY LIKE ANY OTHER

From our modern perspective, knowing that the war would continue for another four years and include three more Christmases, it is tempting to see the 1914 truce as a romanticised 'last chance for peace' before the First World War spiralled into even greater death and destruction. Yet the localised nature of the truce meant that normal fighting continued in other sectors, as recorded by the German officer Lieutenant Fritz Romberg, writing home to his parents on 30 December.

The day before Christmas and over Christmas, our line was hammered with heavy artillery fire (grenades). It went on without pause... In spite of the artillery fire, there stood our soldiers without a complaint, partially in foot-high water, in front and behind them the grenades exploding — but not one of them left his post... Sixty hours the 3rd Battalion held on with a loss of forty dead. But we did celebrate Christmas too. A Christmas tree had been found with difficulty and hundreds of love parcels had arrived. The Evangelium was prayed and afterwards we sang *Ich hat einen Kameraden* ['Once I had a comrade']. With tears in our eyes we went our way again. Personally, I have not received a letter, card or parcel, but we are told that part of the Christmas train is still on the way.

In most areas, therefore, the war carried on as normal. At the very time that the Christmas Truce was happening on the Western Front, British aircraft of the Royal Naval Air Service

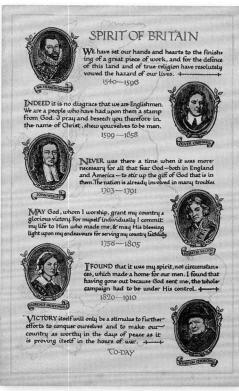

Two examples of embroidered silk postcards produced in France and Belgium for soldiers to send home during the First World War. The vast majority of such cards were commercially mass produced by embroidery machines, but their attractive nature ensured that they were popular wartime momentos.

This Christmas card from the Second World War is remarkably untraditional, featuring quotes from famous Britons including Churchill. The text inside suggests that the message of Christmas 'may mean for all of us a holding to the Faith, living Hopefully towards a victorious peace, in Charity one with another'.

were attacking the German Zeppelin sheds at Cuxhaven in a carefully planned raid. The Allied High Command made every effort to prevent a reoccurrence of the Truce in subsequent years, despite fraternisation and the so-called 'live and let live' mentality sometimes reappearing at other instances throughout the First World War.

The vast majority of soldiers who experienced Christmas during either world war found that it was a day largely like any other, as recognised by Walter Hare of the West Yorkshire Regiment when recalling Christmas 1917.

> They used to say that the fighting stopped for Christmas, well not where we were it didn't. So there were no celebrations. I think it was a bit quiet; there wasn't quite so much shelling going on and that kind of thing. But there wasn't a stop. There wasn't a halt or anything like that. The shelling went on occasionally and the occasional machine-gun and rifle fire, but it was a bit what we would call quiet.

Even spending 25 December in what many would consider the most important Christmas location — Palestine itself — would fail to mark any break to the usual routine, as T G Edgerton

This poster from the First World War promoting the work of the American Red Cross was designed by Edwin Howland Blashfield.

<

In October 1914 the King's daughter, Princess Mary, launched an appeal to raise money to send a Christmas gift to every soldier or sailor serving overseas that year. Different variations of the specially embossed brass or (for officers) silver tins contained a printed greetings card with items such as tobacco, writing equipment or sweets. Around 400,000 were delivered by Christmas 1914.

of the 301st Brigade Royal Field Artillery recalled while stationed just outside Jerusalem in 1917.

Christmas in the Holy Land is a thought many of us have had at some time in our lives. Yet the most miserable Christmas I have ever had, or ever hope to have, was in just this place... We were to take up a position some 800 yards further back. The rain persisted with a piercing cold wind. Those six guns had to be manhandled out of the mud and on to the road before the teams could hook up and take them away. We had no mechanical aid in those days. Drenched to the skin, cold and almost exhausted our guns were eventually in position and we looked in vain for a dry spot to rest. Somebody, somehow, managed to find some tea. The CO ordered a rum ration. Hot tea laced with a small dose of rum and bully beef and biscuits were very welcome Christmas fare. Nobody was in festive mood. In fact I am quite sure nobody realised what the date was until afterwards.

NO REASON TO CELEBRATE

Christmas for those involved in the Second World War would also largely prove little different to any other day, with the more mobile nature of that conflict providing even less chance for occasional fraternisation. Indeed, several Christmas Days during the 1940s proved to be particularly bloodthirsty. Towards the end of the war, the German offensive in the Ardennes region of northern France finally reached its turning point on Christmas Day 1944, resulting in the loss of some 3,500 German troops. And before that, on 25 December 1941, the British colony of Hong Kong had surrendered to Japanese forces following over two weeks of intensive fighting which caused over 5,000 deaths. The hastily scribbled diary entries made by J L A Hardy of the 1st Battalion Middlesex Regiment described their brave but futile defence of the city on Christmas Eve.

There are two thousand Japanese advancing against our small handful of fifty men. This advance position is at the corner of one of the houses. Stationed inside with the Bren gun muzzle ready to fire through the wooden shutters, I am at this moment lying outside observing for enemy movement... Shells are streaking overhead, so close that they land no more than ten yards behind us. In the afternoon we find out that the rest of Z Company HQ have been driven out by the intense shell fire, leaving us alone. The enemy have drawn closer to us and are digging in new positions. They are so close now that I can hear them talking.

Hardy and some 7,000 other British soldiers and civilians were captured and subsequently imprisoned in camps across the Far East. The historic capitulation of Hong Kong became known among the British as 'Black Christmas'.

∧

Following the D-Day invasion of Normandy and the formation of a second European front, the likelihood of a German invasion of Britain was considered unlikely enough to justify the disbandment of the country's Home Guard. This Christmas card marks the Home Guard's formal stand-down in December 1944.

‹

Christmas Day was far from a holiday for many during war. HMS *Hurricane* is photographed being scuttled on 25 December 1943, having been fatally damaged by a German torpedo the day before.

BUSINESS AS USUAL

Even for those troops stationed nearer home, Christmas did not necessarily mean any change to the regular routine, as John Driscoll testified in a letter to his wife at Christmastime 1940. A delay in returning to RAF Gresford after his leave finished on 23 December meant that he was docked pay and confined to barracks for three days. Over 50 men were also found to be absent, and trucks were sent with armed escorts to bring them from their homes.

>

A military postman with his sack of Christmas parcels photographed in Weert, Holland, in November 1944.

I shall never forget last night, Christmas Eve 1940. We sat round a big bin and had to cut and trim about 3 hundredweight of sprouts – yes, sprouts, there were sprouts all round us, some even got in my hair. To crown everything they picked the defaulters for guard. Today (Christmas Day) and I was honoured by being the first name on the list and what a guard we have got. Depot guard, starting at 11am this morning, we are on until 7am the next morning (Boxing Day), 20 hours without being able to take your overcoat and belt off.

> **Troops serving overseas could often find locally produced greetings cards to send home to their families at Christmastime.** This example from the Second World War was made in Italy, despite featuring a very Olde English snowy scene.

Even for those lucky enough to be celebrating Christmas in a more traditional way, war would cause difficulties and frustrations which conspired to make the festive season a challenging one. Shortages of food and resources would impact on civilian life in particular, yet perhaps the biggest hurdle for many seeking to enjoy Christmas during wartime was the challenge of experiencing it alone, without their loved ones close to hand.

British soldiers held captive in Stralsund-Dänholm prisoner of war camp, Germany, were able to send home this specially printed greetings card during the First World War.

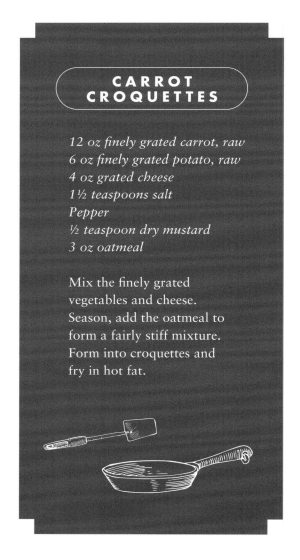

CARROT CROQUETTES

12 oz finely grated carrot, raw
6 oz finely grated potato, raw
4 oz grated cheese
1 ½ teaspoons salt
Pepper
½ teaspoon dry mustard
3 oz oatmeal

Mix the finely grated vegetables and cheese. Season, add the oatmeal to form a fairly stiff mixture. Form into croquettes and fry in hot fat.

Post Christmas letters by

Help Yourself!!

THE RAILWAYS CAN GIVE YOU MUCH BETTER SERVICE DURING THE HOURS OF DAYLIGHT THAN DURING THE BLACKOUT.

IN YOUR OWN INTEREST DECIDE TO TRAVEL BY DAYLIGHT DURING THE CHRISTMAS HOLIDAYS.

SOUTHERN RAILWAY

∧

Postal deliveries grew during both world wars as troops overseas struggled to maintain contact with their loved ones back home. In 1917 over 19,000 mail bags crossed the channel each day. During the Second World War, 'airgraphs' were introduced which enabled multiple messages to be photographed and conveyed by microfilm reel. Christmas meant an even greater demand for the postal service.

∧

Rail travel in Britain during the Second World War could be far from easy at the best of times, due to Air Raid Precaution measures and invasion fears. The added demand from Christmas travellers encouraged rail companies to issue guidance like this.

Separation

CELEBRATING THE
SEASONS APART

For many people, the most difficult aspect of a wartime Christmas was likely spending the festive season apart from their family and friends. During both world wars, many men found themselves fighting overseas in the various branches of the armed forces. Some were perhaps hospitalised with wounds or illness, or held as prisoners of war. Women might also be away in the services or carrying out war work. By the end of both wars, thousands of families had suffered the ultimate separation from loved ones through the death of a family member either in action or from enemy bombing raids. It was rare for a family to survive both global conflicts intact, without at least one fatality among their number.

Separation led to loneliness and homesickness, both common aspects of wartime life. Soldiers such as Ivor Morgan, serving with the 11th Battalion Welsh Regiment in Salonika during the First World War, had to learn how to cope with being so far away from home. This separation was, of course, felt all the more acutely at Christmas time.

PAGE 30
An American GI and WAC (Womens Army Corps) are photographed to promote the Second World War scheme for shared hospitality during Christmastime. Arranged through the Red Cross, it encouraged the sharing of rations and resources.

∧

**Christmas parties on the home front
were often intended to entertain children
separated from their families.** This one,
held at Admiralty House in London on
17 December 1942, was for the children of
naval officers. The small boy being handed
a present happens to be Winston Churchill
Junior, the grandson of the Prime Minister.

∧

**Father Christmas with an orphan child at
a Christmas party organised by the 316th
Troop Carrier Group, part of the United
States Ninth Air Force based in the UK, on
Christmas Day 1944.**

> *Of course we were filled with a nostalgia for home.*

In fact I will confess to you that one practise which I used to use was at night time, when we were out of the line. I used to get away someplace by myself in the darkness, find the direction of the North Star, incline slightly left and think and hope and wish that I were looking towards England. Towards Wales. Towards Neath. And of course my thoughts were of home at that time, but there were many times when I did that. It had no effect, of course, except that I felt I was in contact with my home.

The sorting of Christmas mail is undertaken on board the battleship HMS *King George V*, Christmas Eve 1943.

Christmas parcels destined for British troops serving overseas are sorted at the Army Post Office Home Depot based in Regent's Park, November 1917.

The Second World War would see an even greater opportunity for families to be split up, with huge numbers of children spending Christmas away from their parents and the family home for the first time. As many as 3.5 million British children were evacuated from urban areas considered most likely to suffer from enemy bombing, to be billeted with distant relatives or, just as commonly, complete strangers. Similarly, Jewish children fleeing the persecutions in Germany arrived in the United Kingdom as refugees as a result of the *Kindertransport* scheme at the end of 1939. Every attempt was made by local authorities and charities to provide comfort for such evacuees, and Christmas provided the perfect opportunity to combine such efforts. The 'Phoney War' Christmas of 1939 saw little change for many from the usual celebrations, and it was therefore 1940 which marked the first Christmas of the Second World War to be notably different once the effects of the conflict had made themselves known on everyday life. Children's Christmas parties were arranged, with charitable donations of food and toys helping to bring some seasonal cheer to homesick children.

PARSNIP FRITTERS

2 large parsnips
3 small slices of stale bread
1 teaspoon flour
6 small pieces of bacon
Thick tomato sauce
Pepper and salt
Small piece of margarine

Boil the parsnips until tender. Drain and mash with margarine, pepper and salt. Roll bacon, thread on a skewer and grill. Shape the mashed parsnips into flat cakes with flour. Fry slices of bread and parsnip 'fritters'. Serve the fritters on the fried bread, previously cut into small shapes. The tomato sauce should be served separately.

ISOLATED AWAY
FROM HOME

Such benevolent schemes were all very well on the home front, but charity towards helping those soldiers unfortunate enough to be held captive in enemy hands was far from as straightforward. Harold Browning had been captured during the Fall of Singapore in February 1942, yet by the end of the year had still heard nothing from his family back in Britain. The ability to exchange news with those at home presented the strongest antidote to isolation, and Harold's suspicion that he may have been reported as dead would have been a nagging frustration. At the end of the year, however, a special opportunity was presented to the prisoners.

On 23rd December we were all very excited when it was announced that we could all send cards home, the second since we were made prisoner. This time they were printed and we had to scratch out what didn't apply. Mine went something like this: 'I am in excellent health'. I scratched out 'usual' and 'poor' as I didn't think my health was usual. Neither did I think it was poor considering everything. I also scratched out 'I am in hospital'! After this we were allowed to print ten words of our own and I thought a long time before I chose mine. I finally wrote 'Hoping for news of family. Take care of yourself, darling'. By this I felt that Willie would know that I had not yet heard from her. At the head of the card we had to state No 4 Camp Thailand so we really felt that we might get a reply. We were at any rate telling the people at home where we were.

Naval and marine postmen collecting
Christmas mail at Devonport, 1942.

Even for those families who were lucky enough to be able to maintain a written correspondence despite separation, the pain of being apart from loved ones was always evident. Arthur Harris was serving overseas with the RAF in Secunderabad, India, and 1942 was the first Christmas that he and his wife were to be apart. She set aside time on Christmas Day to write to him.

> My beloved darling, we have just had our Christmas Dinner, and are now listening to *The Fourth Christmas of the War*. I wonder whether you are listening and what you are doing, what you have had for your dinner and how you are spending the day. For my part I'm aching and aching for you, and could just weep if I thought too much about it. Otherwise, darling, I'm reasonably happy and do hope you are and that you are having a good time. I know you will be thinking about me and us all at home, and you know beloved how much we are all thinking about you. I got up first this morning and lit the fire and made the tea, and gave you a big hug and a big kiss before the others came down... I'm now listening to the children in Canada and USA exchanging greetings with their parents; like the silly thing I am, it's making me cry again. There is a postal delivery tomorrow morning although it is Sunday, so I'm eagerly looking for a letter, and if there is one I'll write again tomorrow afternoon.

Christmas cards produced for particular military units were invariably designed with appropriate imagery or jokes, as this explosive example from the First World War illustrates.

Young Derek Cunningham from London's Canning Town receives a Christmas card and gifts, donated by Americans through the British War Relief Society (BWRS) in December 1944. The BWRS was an umbrella organisation which distributed funds from many small charities across the United States.

Communication with home was vital for troops serving overseas. These two Second World War soldiers compare the Christmas cards they have made for their loved ones back home.

BRINGING THE
NATION TOGETHER

One way in which separated friends and family might feel closer to one another was through shared experiences, and radio broadcasts exploited this opportunity by providing programmes which everybody across the globe might wish to enjoy together at the same moment. One such mutual experience which increasingly became associated with Christmas was the royal radio broadcast. This tradition began with King George V in 1932 and soon became an intrinsic part of Christmas Day festivities for many people across the British Empire and later Commonwealth. The BBC's Overseas Service broadcast to the Empire throughout the Second World War, and the royal broadcast was invariably timed for British homes to listen to after what was, for many, the 'main event' of the day – the midday Christmas dinner. In 1941, the Cottrell family from Bromley celebrated Christmas Day like many others in the country, as described by Rose in a letter to her older married sister.

At about 2.15pm we went into the drawing room to listen to the Empire broadcast. I wonder if you listened, I expect you did. We got ready the glasses and drinks at first and at about 2.25pm Dad came in and we had our drinks on time. I hope you did too. Mum of course was popping in and out seeing to the turkey and listening to the programme. Then of course the King came on, and I got quite tensed up when he had such difficulty at first in speaking. However, he got better don't you think in the middle. I expect that broadcast spoilt his whole morning, I expect he was a bundle of nerves, but anyway it was a very good broadcast and the reception all over the Empire was very good.

Land Girl Miss Beatrix Pyne similarly recalled listening to the annual broadcast, this time in 1942, although in her case the monarch's famous speech impediment caused much amusement.

We heard the King's speech on Xmas day, it was just before we went out for milking, and everyone was quiet. I thought of you all at home listening as well, and when I thought of old Gert, and then the King said something about 'Twabwuk' [Tobruk] and 'countwy' [country]. I burst out giggling and made out it was something else making me laugh. I laughed again when he mentioned the land workers and was glad when the thing was over.

Perched on a ladder, a sailor writes home from HMS *Dunluce Castle*, part of the Home Fleet, in December 1941. The ship also happened to serve as the main mail sorting depot for the fleet.

> This poster advertises an event from Christmas 1915 in which photographic postcards were sold in aid of the National Fund for Welsh Troops. Christmas was the perfect occasion on which to hang such charitable causes.

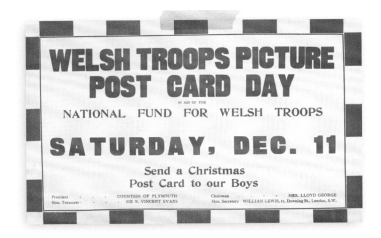

< This 1915 Christmas card designed for the Black Watch looks forward to successes in 1916. Yet two of the regiment's battalions serving in France would suffer losses during the Battle of the Somme, while another would be involved in the disastrous Siege of Kut in Mesopotamia.

Doing their part in furthering international relations, a soldier of the Machine Gun Corps kisses a French farm girl under a sprig of mistletoe near Hesdin, France, on 20 December 1917.

Shortages

MAINTAINING TRADITIONS

During both world wars, Christmas luxuries could be hard to come by. Although shortages were prevalent during the First World War due to the German submarine campaign which sought to starve the British isles into submission, food rationing and other restrictions really made themselves known most stridently during the Second World War, with the government-promoted notion of 'make do and mend' encouraging people to make the most out of what limited resources were available. This became particularly evident at Christmastime, when gifts exchanged were often homemade and practical ones, while children's toys were commonly made from recycled materials or whatever resources happened to be at hand. As we shall see in a subsequent chapter, inventiveness was also essential in order to find substitutes for the key festive ingredients for Christmas dinners.

Despite the limited resources at their disposal, many people still made the effort to realize their annual traditions. During the First World War, nurse Margaret Callender put a special effort into decorating the 22nd American Red Cross Hospital in London where she worked.

That was my happy time! I did all the decorations for my ward, anyhow. Two Christmases I was there and did that. The other nurses helped me, you know, but I had to devise it all. We had very big mantle pieces and in the winter time I made a cottage with snow on top and light inside, windows and so on. And on the dark blue blinds I made a night sky, I had little polar bears and things in front and snow and little huts, too. And I put stars on the dark window, you see. And I think all the lights were snow drops.

During the same war, Louie Johnson ensured that each of the patients at her hospital in Leeds received a Christmas present. Charity came to the fore at Christmastime.

People would kindly come in and give me little presents for the men, or money to buy presents. And I used to go to Leeds and make a little gift parcel for every man. Usually a packet of cigarettes, tobacco pouch, perhaps a scarf if they were going out, or an ounce of tobacco or something like that. And give every man a little present on Christmas morning, every time.

PAGE 46
A group of young children at Fen Ditton Junior School, Cambridgeshire, design and make their own paper chain Christmas decorations in December 1944.

︿
This linocut was designed by German internee Hellmuth Weissenborn for Christmas 1940. He was interned in Hutchinson camp on the Isle of Man, often known as 'the artists camp' due to the thriving artistic community within its walls.

Father Christmas lifts a young girl up to look at a toy soldier on the Christmas tree at a home for evacuees in Henley-on-Thames, Oxfordshire, in 1941. Interestingly, this Father Christmas is actually played by a woman, perhaps indicating the shortages of menfolk on the home front!

GREETINGS CARDS

Seasonal greetings were traditionally exchanged through the sending of Christmas cards. These were still a relatively new phenomenon during the First World War, having only been circulated widely in the previous few decades due to the introduction of cheap printing processes. Typical imagery featured on cards included rustic scenes of snow and nostalgia which appealed to those serving overseas by providing a reminder of the normal, peaceful life they were notionally fighting to retain.

Paper shortages grew more evident during the Second World War, meaning that things like Christmas cards became increasingly scarce. Those that were obtainable tended to be printed on flimsy paper and were small in size, with the best examples often being retained for reuse in subsequent years. In 1941, to conserve paper, the Ministry of Supply

This 1944 Christmas card designed for No 4 Survey Regiment of the British Liberation Army depicts Father Christmas finding some appropriate surveying equipment in his sack.

decreed that 'no retailer shall provide any paper for the packing or wrapping of goods excepting food stuffs or articles which the shopkeeper has agreed to deliver.' This made it difficult to keep Christmas presents a surprise, yet newsprint often served as an alternative wrapping. Coloured paper was very rare and much sought after, but if obtained could provide the basis for homemade garlands made from cut out patterns strung up with string.

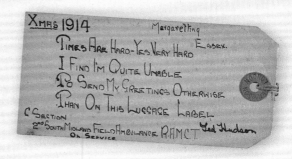

> **This Second World War Christmas card serves as a useful reminder of the various branches and responsibilities encompassed by Britain's home front Civil Defence organisation.**

> **This festive message, written on a luggage label and dating from the first Christmas of the First World War, perhaps indicates the novelty factor still apparent at the beginning of the conflict.** Troops would often send souvenirs home from their service overseas.

CUTTING-DOWN FOR THE CHILDREN

Here are ideas for turning grown-up's discarded garments into children's clothes:

BATHING WRAPS
can be made into children's dressing gowns.

GREY FLANNEL TROUSERS
will make children's knickers and skirts.

MACKINTOSHES
will cut down for a child's waterproof coat or cape with pixie hood to match.

PLUS-FOURS
would make two pairs of shorts for a schoolboy.

PYJAMA LEGS
will make children's vests.

AN OLD SKIRT
will make one pair of knickers and a little play-skirt for a seven-year old.

VEST AND COMBINATION TOPS
will make bodices on to which a little girl's skirt or a small boy's knickers will button.

WASHING-SILK DRESSES
make up into gay pyjamas for children.

WOOLLEN STOCKINGS
with worn feet can have the legs opened down the back seams and can then be made up into an infant's jersey. Bind it with ribbon at neck, sleeves and hem.

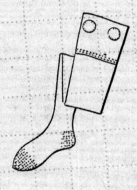

CHRISTMAS PRESENTS

Shortages of goods in the shops obviously affected the staple seasonal activity of gift shopping, yet other restrictions added to the mix to make a Christmas shopping trip particularly novel during wartime. In December 1940, the German bombing raids on England were at their most intense, and the air raid precautionary measures in place meant that Christmas took on a very different character for shoppers such as Rose Cottrell from Bromley, Kent.

Christmas shopping in the blackout is the most terrible business of all, especially when one does not know what to buy. Of course the crowds in the High Street are awful, and one keeps bumping into people and falling off the pavement, and getting tied up with dogs, and in the drizzle of course some people had

umbrellas up and they were death traps. It is impossible to look in shop windows once the blackout starts. We arrived back about 6.30pm with not much to show for our pains.

Based fairly nearby in central London, Mrs E J Barnicot shared Rose's frustrations at the difficulties of wartime shopping.

>

A typical children's Christmas stocking, circa 1940. Simply made toys and puzzles made from wood and paper were common during wartime.

I went to Peter Jones yesterday and got some toys for the children for christmas.

I shopped under difficulties as there were incessant raid warnings and we had to go down to the basement and back again. The roof spotter rings a violent bell and the lights are turned off and everybody marches to the exits and proceeds to the basements and sit on the second-hand furniture till the danger is past.

'MAKE DO AND MEND'

Christmas shopping, of course, was no longer possible for those troops or civilians who would be spending Christmas behind wire. Following the German invasion of the Channel Islands in June 1940, residents were gradually transferred to internment camps in Germany. Based in Schloss Wurzach near the most southerly German border, Mrs Coles and her fellow internees still celebrated Christmas as best they could, with parties arranged for the children and dances for the adults. But each year the celebrations and the makeshift toys and gifts became more and more austere. Their first experience of Christmas while interned was in 1942.

We awoke at 5.30am this Christmas morn, to hear the first of 19 children discovering what Father Christmas had put into their small stockings! Gradually the voices rose to a crescendo until all 19 children were laughing and talking at once. Fragments from Red Cross parcels, bits of material made into quaint animals and numerous little wooden toys, all made in the camp, helped to make this day as happy as possible for the children. All rooms were gaily decorated with crepe paper, chains and bright festoons, mostly obtained from Red Cross parcels, and some had been passed in by the German guards. Christmas trees were brought in from the village and placed in the larger rooms, where they were later trimmed with small gifts of chocolates, cigarettes and hand-made articles. A children's party was held in the Theatre from 2pm—4.30pm. Father Christmas was present and gave each child a packet of sweets. Prizes, supplied by the Red Cross, were given for various competitions. Bread and butter, cake and tea at 4.30pm!

This handmade Father Christmas doll was sewn by Lance Corporal Charles Frampton, while hospitalised during the First World War. It was given to his young sister as a Christmas present.

During a spare moment in September 1943, Stoker W Church, of Laindon in Essex, makes money boxes decorated with famous Disney characters. Such homemade toys would likely end up in a child's Christmas stocking that year.

CHRISTMAS DECORATIONS

Decorating one's home for the season has always been a popular aspect of Christmas, and the changes instituted to civilian life by conflict in the early twentieth century meant that, for the Second World War in particular, it was not just living rooms and dining rooms that were filled with decorations. As we have seen, even prison camps were decorated for Christmas. Back on the home front where fears of enemy bombing were making themselves known, many people equipped their house's cellar as an air raid shelter or buried corrugated iron Anderson shelters in their garden. In an attempt to bring Christmas cheer to even the most dreary situations, people like Viola Bawtree decided to decorate their shelter.

I've trailed ivy and glitter down the sides of the cellar stairs, and pinned up some very old Xmas cards sent me when a baby. How queer it all seems! No warning yet, 7.15pm, so I'm alone down here... I've decorated the little tree but shall have to grope for it in the dark tomorrow as breakfast will be before light.

Viola's experiences in Surrey in 1940 were typical of those living in areas of the country liable to experience enemy bombing. Christmas Day itself dawned, following a quiet night.

We walked to church down Brighton Road but walked back via Langley Park, and Sylvia conducted the tour by pointing out where bombs had fallen, and we stopped and looked at a demolished house with only the staircase left above the ground floor.

Decorating the Christmas Tree, December 1944 by John Worsley. The Red Cross crate pictured immediately in front of the Christmas tree indicates that the two figures are decorating their hut in a prisoner of war camp.

A most depressing walk home! It did seem strange when we walked to Church to see Sylvia, Hilda, Ivan and JA all with their gas masks slung on their backs. I looked out for others and saw none at all. I wonder if they were the only ones who took them? When I told Hilda she said the Government asked everyone to carry them and she felt it only right to do as they asked.

Athel and Daisy and Shirley to dinner, but they had to get away at 4pm to get ready for their dug out before dark! Very nice dinner. No fruit or nuts or anything afterwards, and tea at 5pm. I stayed in dining room to be sociable instead of coming down here [in the cellar] where I longed to be, and watched them play at drawing a beetle by dice throwing... It's the first evening I've spent above cellar since the raids began in this neighbourhood. I believe we could sleep in our beds tonight, but I prefer it down here!

SWEDE SOUP

2 pints stock or water
1¼ lb swedes, peeled
* and shredded*
2 oz onion, chopped
Salt and pepper to taste
2 level tablespoons flour
4 tablespoons milk
2 level tablespoons
* chopped parsley*

Put the water or stock in a pan and bring to the boil. When boiling, add the shredded swedes, onion and seasoning. Boil for 20 minutes. Mix the flour to a smooth paste with a little water. Add to the soup and re-boil, stirring to prevent lumps. Cook for 5 minutes. Add the milk and re-heat but do not boil. Stir in the parsley just before serving.

Captured Allied officers pose for the camera in Colditz castle, December 1941.
Colditz prisoner of war camp in southern Germany, designated Oflag IV-C, held particularly troublesome officers.

THE CHRISTMAS TREE

One of the most potent emblems of the festive season remains the Christmas tree, its origins dating from pagan times with the evergreen representing the continuation of life throughout winter. The tradition of dressing a tree was particularly popular in Germany, but endorsement by the British royal family in 1848 meant that decorated trees were soon adopted in Britain and by the First World War were a well-established tradition. Timber shortages during the Second World War, however, meant that Christmas trees became increasingly difficult to obtain. Replica trees were therefore sometimes adopted or potted trees reused from previous years. Viola Bawtree's potted tree reappeared in 1941, yet she took the opportunity on that occasion to create another decorative addition. This was intended as a gift for the German refugee Mr Assenheim who

was lodging in her home, separated from his wife due to the war.

I cut some bushy twigs from a little cupressus tree and set them in a small pot. Then I wired some of the branches, and fixed seven tiny candles (birthday cake candles cut in half) each in a beech nut case painted green inside. On wee flags cut from red and green ribbon I painted our names, and hung one from each candle. The candles were in little holders made of thin tin, and fixed in the nut case with melted candle grease. The two at the very top of the tree were named for him and his wife. I painted empty walnut shells with gold paint, tucked some postage stamps in and tied the halves together with green ribbon. These, with some sweets and a pencil, were the only ornaments, but the tree looked very pretty, and the main idea of it was that it should be a Wish-Tree.

We gathered round the tea-table after dark on Boxing Day, switching off the light while Mr Assenheim lighted the tiny candles. As we watched them burn we all thought of those two so sadly separated from each other, and hoped, and wished, and prayed for their reunion and for their welfare. And as we watched the tiny twinkling lights in the darkened room, Mr Assenheim, standing at the head of the table, started singing that beautiful 'Holy Night' tune. Neither he nor any of us knew the words, but we all joined in softly, and it seemed the one tune more suitable than any other for such an occasion; reverend, peaceful and lovely. As the candles continued burning we sang it through a second time. Then one by one they flickered out, and the ceremony was over. But later in the evening we put the record of the song on to the gramophone; the tree was still on the table, and as I listened I looked up at the two empty candle-holders at the top and thought again of those two who were so sadly separated from each other.

Representing life and growth during wintertime as well as lighting up the darkness, the Christmas tree remains a dominant image. It is easy to see how the reliable evergreen symbol came to represent, for those living through the war, a symbol of defiance over the destruction and chaos caused by conflict. The Blitz on British cities lasted throughout December 1940 and into the new year, with the particularly intensive bombing of the capital on the night of 29—30 December inflicting what became known as 'the Second Great Fire of London'. The morning after, Leslie Smith walked through the streets of the City to witness the destruction and was amazed at what he saw when approaching London's largest cathedral.

The Spirit of Britain we hear so much about was epitomised in the Christmas tree on the top step of the entrance to St Paul's with fairy lights bravely competing against a glow of more sinister import. Such is London — carrying on as before — wounded, but fighting back.

A member of the Women's Auxiliary Service, 2nd Polish Corps, decorates a Christmas tree on 12 December 1944.

THE MOST SERIOUS SHORTAGE?

Perhaps the most unusual wartime shortage mostly affected those in captivity during the war. With food and luxuries being increasingly rare as the war progressed, the other most notable aspect usually lacking from life behind the wire was an absence of the opposite sex. Male prisoners of war would rarely see a woman throughout their entire time in captivity, while men and women were usually held in separate internment camps, particularly in the Far East. However, Christmas 1942 would present a special opportunity for those interned in Singapore's Changi Gaol.

The Japanese relaxed the ban on the sexes for two hours on Christmas Day, i.e. from 10—12 midday the doors and gates separating the male and female portions of the gaol were opened and those who had invitations from the women's camp were allowed in. If you realise that for eight solid months the majority of us here have not spoken to a woman beyond possibly on occasional 'hello, how are you' spoken from a distance, this concession meant a lot. Armed with an invitation card which had to be produced to our own camp police at the door or gate of admission, we were duly ushered in and sat down to small tables or benches and consumed coffee (real) and small cakes (homemade at some difficulty). Of course we talked at 19 to the dozen and many of the women seemed very excited. The meeting of husbands and wives was sometimes pathetic to see. Every man in the camp had a 'present' from the ladies, even if it was only a 2 cent native cheroot. This was a kindly thought and involved a deal of work on their part. Of course only a very limited number of men could go across, as excluding the Eurasian community over there, there cannot be more than about 100 white women all told.

Such novel situations and surprising changes to the norm were appropriate staples of Christmastime, although one of the most important aspects of Christmas affected by the restrictions imposed by war was arguably food. In particular, the traditional Christmas dinner.

ONION, TOMATO AND HARICOT BAKE

4 oz haricot beans
1 lb onions
2 oz flour
½ pint milk
½ pint onion water
2 oz grated cheese
2 level teaspoons salt
½ level teaspoon pepper
¼ teaspoon
  dry mustard
8 oz sliced or
  bottled tomatoes

Wash the beans and soak overnight; cook until tender and drain. Peel, cut up and boil the onions until tender; strain and save the liquor. Make a sauce with the flour, milk and onion water, and add the grated cheese and seasoning. Arrange the onions, tomatoes and beans in layers in a pie dish (2 pint size), cover with the sauce and bake in a hot oven for 15–20 minutes.

BUY A
CHRISTMAS PRESENT
FOR YOUR SOLDIER FRIEND.

A PIPE OR A POUCH WILL
BE WELCOME.

Don't Forget Him!

ROYAL ALBERT HALL
MANAGER   HILTON CARTER
GRAND
CHRISTMAS FAIR
Wed & Thur. Nov. 29th & 30th

IN AID OF
"OUR DUMB FRIENDS' LEAGUE"
SPECIAL FUNDS AND INSTITUTIONS INCLUDING
THE BLUE CROSS FUND.
Tickets: Afternoon 2/6.: Evening (after 5 p.m.) 1/- DOORS OPEN 11 a.m.
A VOUCHER will be attached to each ticket
entitling the holder to purchase goods to the value.

ARTHUR J. COKE, Organiser & Secretary
58 Victoria Street, LONDON, S.W.

∧

**This advertisement encouraging
Christmas generosity dates from the First
World War.** The commercialism recognised
as part of our modern version of the festive
holiday was apparent even in this earlier era.

∧

**The larger wartime charities organised
significant fund-raising events, such as
this Christmas Fair during the First World
War in aid of the Blue Cross animal charity.**

Food

CHRISTMAS DINNER

A large part of the Christmas tradition is the festive feast, usually consisting of large quantities of the very best quality food complemented by copious alcoholic drink. One's ability to enjoy a good meal or drink is invariably linked to overall feelings of happiness, and it is therefore not so surprising that those living through the two world wars would often attach greatest importance during the festive period to making sure a good dinner was enjoyed. With wartime rationing making itself known during both conflicts, however, it could be a challenge to overcome such restrictions and shortages.

For those serving in the armed forces, Christmas food tended to be better than the usual rations issued throughout the rest of the year. During the First World War, Frederick Higgins had fond memories of enjoying an important part of the Christmas menu.

It didn't matter where you were, there was a ration of Christmas pudding for you every Christmas. I'd be scooping it out with a spoon out of the tins; they were big tins holding about seven pounds, I suppose, all specially made. If somebody said you've got to have a bit of Christmas pudding, no doubt I would, I must say, speaking for myself! We had Christmas pudding every Christmas. I can't remember what we had to eat, what the dinner was, but we certainly had afters!

Others were not so lucky, such as 2nd Lieutenant William Richards who recalled the awful winter of Christmas 1916 on the Western Front.

My Christmas dinner was a tin of bully beef which I'd dug out of the snow, because it had been discarded by the previous occupants of the gun pit. The cook, he made a hash of it, you know what I mean. He just fried it up and made a hash of it.

POTATO PIGLETS

6 medium well-scrubbed potatoes
6 skinned sausages
Cooked cabbage, lightly chopped

Remove a centre core, using an apple corer, from the length of each potato, and stuff the cavity with sausage meat. Bake in the usual way and arrange the piglets on a bed of cooked cabbage. (The potato removed from each is useful for soup.)

PAGE 66
Junior ratings get their first taste of the Christmas pudding being made at the Royal Naval Barracks Devonport, November 1940.

A tank crew of the 44th Battalion, Royal Tank Regiment, part of the 4th Armoured Brigade, unpack a Christmas parcel to reveal a pudding inside. What may at first appear to be a Christmas tree behind them is, in fact, their camouflaged tank.

SIXPENCE
MEANS A
HAPPY SOLDIER

Every Sixpence given to the Fund
Will supply <u>one</u> Soldier
With his piece of Pudding
On Christmas Day.
<u>Three million</u> men have to be provided
  for,
So there is much to be done,
And help is required—from <u>everyone</u>.
<u>You</u> will enjoy
<u>Your</u> Christmas Pudding
Much better if you <u>know</u>
That you have made
At least <u>one</u> of the men
Fighting for you in the Trenches
Happy on Christmas Day.

A Christmas dinner being prepared in the
front line, 19 December 1944.

This charitable endeavour from the First
World War recognises the importance of
food to a soldier's happiness - particularly
during the Christmas season.

SEASONAL TRADITIONS

It was a common military and naval tradition that at Christmas time the officers served the men their Christmas dinner. William Holmes, a private in the London Regiment, thoroughly enjoyed this arrangement. His unit were based at Poperinghe in Belgium for Christmas 1917, having just come out of the line for a period of rest.

For two days, starting off the first morning, the officers and sergeants came round and brought us our early morning tea, breakfast, dinner, tea and everything, the whole two days. We never had one parade those whole two days. And we were treated as though we were the officers. Every officer and every sergeant spent the whole of his time bringing us food and smokes and that. All smoking away, singing away, food galore. It was the only time, I shall never forget.

But John Wainwright found that such a custom had its drawbacks.

On this Christmas Day, I was one of the NCOs looking after the men. And I remember we were very, very busy indeed. The men, I believe, they had a very good meal. I just can't remember if it was turkey or roast pork or whatever it was. But it was a traditional Christmas meal, a very good meal indeed. Then afterwards, we were supposed to have our meal in the cookhouse afterwards. But by the time we got there, all the food had gone and I missed my Christmas dinner! So that's one of my memories of Christmas Day.

Christmas dinner is enjoyed by officers in the wardroom of HMS *Malaya* at Scapa Flow, 25 December 1942

MEALS FOR THOSE
BACK HOME

Civilian life also had its challenges for those trying to celebrate Christmas through a decent meal, with wartime food rationing being the most notable factor which impinged upon the traditional Christmas dinner. This was not so much of a problem during the First World War, as compulsory rationing of foodstuffs was not imposed until 1918, the final year of the war. Butter, margarine, lard, sugar and meat were all rationed, with restrictions placed on the amounts which could be eaten in public places. In terms of celebrating a Christmas meal in one's home, however, the careful setting aside of the important ingredients and saving of ration coupons throughout the year meant that people could still generally ensure the delivery of a better-than-usual festive dinner. For unfortunates such as Walter Griffin, however,

imprisoned in Canterbury Prison in 1917 for his conscientious objection to the war, every day was the same.

Christmas Day was no different from any other; of course, war was on and in any case prison isn't a place where they want to make any amusements, things very joyful for you. As far as eats are concerned, well the food was exactly the same as any other day. I presume the kitchen would have been quite pleased it was no different, because they could do it with their eyes shut in any case. And on Christmas Day I know for sure the menu — haha! That sounds good doesn't it? — in the hotel that I was enjoying then was soup, potatoes, bread and rice. The quantities were more or less very carefully allowed out so that there were no second helpings, of course!

The Second World War would present a greater challenge. Rationing of commodities such as bacon, butter and sugar was introduced from January 1940, while meat, tea, biscuits, cheese, eggs, lard, milk and canned or dried fruit would soon follow. By August 1942, almost all food was rationed in some way, with the exception of vegetables and bread. Fruit often enjoyed at Christmas such as lemons and bananas became largely unobtainable, although oranges continued to be sold primarily to children and pregnant women. As during the First World War, many people chose to save particular foodstuffs in preparation for special events such as birthday or Christmas celebrations, while government pamphlets offered advice on how best to create enticing recipes using only the most basic ingredients. As it was, it was estimated in 1943 that only 10 per cent of the population would, that year, enjoy a traditional Christmas dinner.

Christmas Day in the Galley by John Worsley, 1941.

A British soldier appears pleased to
receive this canned Christmas pudding
at snow-covered Neulette, France, on
17 December 1917.

NEW LIFE FOR OLD WOOLLIES

JUMPERS.
Re-knit the sleeves, in stripes, using up oddments of brightly-coloured wool, and make the new shaping at the top, thus giving it an extended shoulder-line. Add a striped pocket to match. A discarded jumper will make a child's jersey or frock. A 2-ply jumper in a pale colour would re-knit into a vest.

GOLF STOCKINGS.
Re-knit worn golf stockings into serviceable socks.

WORN SLEEVES.
Unpick at the shoulder seams, and put in new sleeves knitted in a contrasting colour or, using the best part of the old wool with some new, knit in stripes, panels or a half-and-half design. If the elbows alone are worn, cut them off above the damaged part, and bind with contrasting petersham braid, ribbon or material from the bit bag, cut on the cross. Add a similar binding at the neckline to give a finish. An Old Skirt. Re-knit into a cardigan or jacket for an adult or into two jerseys for a child.

HAND-KNITTED SOCKS AND STOCKINGS.
Unravel these when they are worn and knit them up again into ankle socks. Unravelled tops could be knitted on to other tops to make new feet. The tops of a pair of wool stockings will make cosy underpants for a small boy.

USE FOR A MAN'S WAISTCOAT.
A man's discarded waistcoat can be made into a woman's jerkin by knitting a woollen back and sleeves. Beige with chocolate-brown, or canary coloured sleeves and back on a black pin-striped waistcoat would be very effective.

SHARING DURING THE SEASON

Sharing a meal with loved ones is traditionally an important part of Christmas, yet wartime duty often made this difficult or even impossible. The best alternative, therefore, was to share with those around you – whether friends, neighbours, fellow soldiers, hospital patients or captives. Such sharing was actually encouraged by food rationing anyway, which promoted the value of pooling resources in order to make the most of what limited ingredients might be available.

Special effort was made to feed those in most need, with hospitalised troops in particular feeling the benefit of extra food at Christmastime. Laurence Reynolds was suffering from a double dose of malaria and typhoid, and receiving treatment in a hospital in New Delhi when Christmas 1942 came round.

Sisters and the patients decorated the ward with Indian flowering shrubs and leaves, paper chains, balloons and an improvised Christmas tree. The festive atmosphere was enhanced by carols on the radio. What a strange Christmas Eve!

Christmas morning does not stop the ritual at 5.30am of taking one's temperature and pulse and the question 'bowels open?' Surprised and delighted to have a hearty breakfast of eggs, bacon and sausage instead of our usual diet. Had Communion (brought to us in bed) in morning. Spent morning listening to radio. The next surprise was that we were allowed to have the Christmas dinner – turkey, ham, sausages, roast potatoes and veg, followed

An Italian woman and her children help British troops to pluck turkeys for Christmas dinner, December 1917.

by Christmas pudding with brandy sauce, mince pies, jelly and blancmange, fruit, nuts and sweets. I was even allowed a bottle of beer! Crackers, smoking and yarning followed, until tea time,

Even those serving in the most remote locations sought to celebrate Christmas appropriately with special feasting. Captain M F Carver was serving in Greece as the Special Operations Executive liaison officer with the Greek People's Liberation Army, and December 1943 was to be spent in the mountains. Yet efforts were still made to make the occasion as pleasurable as possible.

For Christmas, all austerities were forgotten. A merchant appeared who intended to make a trip to Athens and Paul gave him his orders. 'Two dozen champagne, two dozen red wine, almonds, raisins, sweets.' An enormous bill soon mounted up to be paid in sovereigns on the black market. We were deviating in a good cause in consuming supplies which the voracious Teuton would eat otherwise. But Christmas Day 1943 was something of a flop. The snow was there alright, but when we sat down to a real breakfast, porridge and bacon and eggs, the porridge was full of weevils. At dinner that night bottles were opened with

suitable pops and healths were drunk. After that, the party became rather quiet as strong men tried to persuade protesting stomachs to accept the windy and chemical enormities that those bottles had contained. The red wine was not quite so nauseating as the champagne. So we were glad to fall back on the familiar Uzo and a large bottle of Krasi we had got from Deskati.

Christmas Day in the London Bridge YMCA Canteen by Clare Atwood, 1920.
The flags of the Allied nations hang above the canteen as festive bunting.

CHRISTMAS IN CAPTIVITY

Prisoners of war and civilian internees in particular struggled to create a traditional Christmas dinner, often relying on the contents of the much-valued food parcels sent from the Red Cross. British prisoners of the Japanese were particularly frustrated in their attempts to feast in a traditional fashion, as Harold Browning observed in 1942.

My first Christmas as a POW began with breakfast of the usual rice porridge and a small spoon of sugar. Some wag put up our usual tiffin menus on the notice-board as follows: Consommé Jungle, Rice Ecossasi, Mince pie, Tea. The first item was the usual vegetable stew, the second was the usual rice, the third was an unheard of thing for tiffin and consisted of a rice pasty with a little pumpkin jam inside and the last was very much the usual tea... The dinner menu was a good deal better than the tiffin and appeared as follows on the notice-board: Consommé Wampo, Rice a la Ande, Boar a la Santa Claus, Crackling Wenceslas, Thai Pie. Being interpreted this meant pork stew and rice with crackling and a pork pasty. Half starved as we were, it tasted wonderful and most of us came back for 'lagis', some even a third and fourth time as there was so much left over. [The Japanese] gave each man some peanut butter and rice toffee as an Xmas present. We couldn't understand such generosity on their part until we actually opened some of the packets and saw they were full of weevils. We ate them just the same. The river was dynamited for fish in the afternoon and so some lucky people had fish as well for their dinner.

A group of British captives stand with the Red Cross parcels they have been sent for Christmas at Yokohama prisoner of war camp, Japan, in 1943.

OCCUPATION AND AUSTERITY

While food rationing made Christmas celebrations difficult in Britain during the Second World War, the availability of food within Germany and parts of occupied Europe grew increasingly scarce as the end of the conflict approached. For most, the armistice when it came did not automatically mean a return to normality. Indeed, for those within the Allied zones of occupation, Christmas 1945 was characterised by severe austerity, as Squadron Leader Richard Leven witnessed in Berlin.

It must have been a grim Christmas for the Germans. The food situation was appalling. The population were living in overcrowded conditions because the Army and RAF had requisitioned nearly every sizable building. We had every facility to enjoy ourselves.

Wine flowed and parties were given. Geraldo and his band played energetically and the bar was kept open. I was unable to be happy because of the knowledge that people living in the same town had been reduced to a state of utter misery. I felt we should have made some effort to help them enjoy their Christmas. At least we could have given a party for the children. I suggested the idea to higher authority, but it was scoffed at. I was told that any army of occupation had no intention of giving a party for the children of a conquered race.

Men of the 20th Hussars pictured with a chicken which they have bought for their Christmas dinner at Bailleul, on the Western Front, December 1916. Each man has a sprig of festive mistletoe stuck in his cap.

MOCK GOOSE

1 lb salted cod
1 tablespoon flour
  or 1½ tablespoons
  national
flour
Pepper
1 tablespoon sage
1–2 onions or leeks
4–6 potatoes
1 cup water or
  pot liquor
2 tablespoons dripping
1 teaspoon vinegar

Tear skin from cod using a knife, wash thoroughly. Place in a pan the skinned side down with just sufficient cold water to cover and ½ teaspoon sugar. Bring slowly to boiling point and allow to simmer 3 minutes. Pour off the water. Remove bone and cut cod into convenient-sized pieces. Mix flour with pepper and sage. Slice onions or leeks finely; peel and slice potatoes. Dip the cod in the seasoned flour and arrange in layers in a dish or tin with the onions and potatoes, leaving a layer of potatoes on top. Add the pot liquor, dot with dripping, and bake in a moderate oven for ¾–1 hour.

Alternatively, heat the fat in a frying pan, arrange the ingredients as above, add the water, cover with a lid or plate, and cook steadily for ½–¾ hour. Brown underneath just before serving.

It was not uncommon for regimental Christmas cards to poke fun at the enemy. This one, issued to the 11th Infantry Division for Christmas 1917, draws attention to the most important gift that soldiers might enjoy in the trenches.

This German poster from 1917 displays many of the same patriotic sentiments as shown in posters from the Allied nations. The text reads: 'Thanks from the Kaiser and People to the Army and Navy / Christmas gift 1917' and appears to have been linked to an appeal for Hamburg retailers to provide comforts to the troops.

Ruhleben civilian internment camp in Germany boasted an impressive printing press, allowing the creation of professional Christmas cards and magazines during the First World War. This example was a joint Christmas message, likely from the merchant ship captains held there.

THE SEASON OF GOODWILL

However, the end of the Second World War meant that reconciliation with one's enemies was a possibility for the first time, and what better occasion for this than at Christmas? Now was the time to forget one's differences and share in the joy and goodwill of the season. 1946 saw the 12 year old Jim Oakes spending Christmas Day with his aunt and uncle at their home in Harold Wood, but his father was about to spring a surprise on the family by offering an impromptu invitation to Christmas dinner to a German resident of the nearby prisoner of war camp.

As Dad ushered him into the room we were confronted with a very apprehensive and obviously very scared, frail looking, middle aged man whose bewilderment was very apparent. My father, who had never given a thought to the communication problem, made a valiant effort to introduce this stranger to his family. Uncle Fred put a glass of port into his hand, us boys stood there with our mouths open, Mum and Aunty Doris returned to the kitchen, shaking their heads, to find an extra plate. After this initial introduction, where we found out that the German's name was Erich, a Christmas toast was proposed. When Erich had drained his glass he was ready to leave and thanked everybody profusely. Dad tried telling him that he was to stay for dinner but Erich would have none of it. Anybody knowing my father's power of persuasion would know that Erich did stop for Christmas dinner; whether he enjoyed that meal is doubtful but we all did try to make him feel welcome

CHRISTMAS PUDDINGS FOR SOLDIERS & SAILORS

SPECIAL COLLECTION FOR THE "SHEFFIELD TELEGRAPH" FUND.

(APPROVED BY THE ARMY COUNCIL.)

To provide Christmas Puddings for Soldiers in all the War Areas, and Naval Men serving with the Expeditionary Force; the Wounded in all Hospitals; and for men on Mine Sweepers, Trawlers, Patrol Boats, and other Naval units.

Letter from SIR DOUGLAS HAIG: General Headquarters, British Armies in France—"On behalf of those whose Christmas will be made brighter by your kindness, I wish to thank you."—D. HAIG. General.

PLEASE PUT YOUR CONTRIBUTION IN THE BOX ON THE PLATFORM.

This poster, asking for charitable donations to be put towards providing Christmas puddings for the troops, would have been displayed at railway stations. It requests that money be deposited 'in the box on the platform'.

After dinner Erich made it clear that he had to return to the camp. As he shook hands and made his farewell, tears filled his eyes. He turned and walked up the path. A frail man with a big POW across his back.

Over the next few months, the Oakes family maintained regular contact with Erich until he was able to return home to Germany. They would continue to exchange greetings with him every subsequent Christmas, in remembrance of their two families being brought together by the consequences of war and the friendship fostered by Christmas.

THE DEPÔT
...SONAL COMFORTS
FOR
...UNDED SOLDIERS
AT
...FFIELD HOSPITALS

...T OF REQUIREMENTS
...RGENTLY NEEDED

...N CAKES.   GAMES.
...S.   FRUITS.
...MALADE.   VEGETABLES.
...S.   SAUSAGES.
...IT   POLONIES.
...C   CIGARETTES.
...   ...CHES.

ROYAL
INFIRMARY
60 MEN
A
Happy
Xmas

Part of the Christmas gifts, mainly of food, collected and distributed through the Leicester Mail's 'Santa Claus Fund' in 1914. The signs in the background indicate the gifts were destined for 'wounded soldiers at Sheffield hospitals'.

Entertainment

One familiar element of the shared Christmas experience is entertainment, whether through the singing of carols and popular songs, party games after a hearty dinner, or the peculiarly British tradition of the pantomime performance. Above all, the emphasis should be upon fun and the seasonal prominence given to children and childlike happiness encourages a wide variety of pursuits and distractions. Homespun and community-based entertainment were particularly relevant during the era of the First World War, before television and radio became commonplace within homes, while by the Second World War the wireless had become integral to everyday life. But during both conflicts it was often up to individuals, families and groups to make their own entertainment, a tradition already strong within the armed forces.

PAGE 94

In December 1943, Admiral Sir Lionel Wells, the Commanding Officer Orkney and Shetlands, was presented with a special Christmas gift by the Russian Admiral Arseniy Golovko. Quite what he decided to do with the three-month old reindeer Olga is not recorded.

L

Members of the Womens Royal Naval Service (WRNS) put on a Christmas pantomime performance of Cinderella. Chief Officer Nye appears as the Fairy Godmother, while 2nd Officer Wood is being drawn by the horse!

TOP IMAGE

The Christmas gang show was a popular form of entertainment within the armed forces. This hula dance is being performed by three members of the ship's company from a Royal Navy destroyer based at Scapa Flow, 18 December 1942.

MIDDLE IMAGE

A behind-the-scenes photograph from the same ship's Christmas show. A considerable amount of effort went into such entertainments.

BOTTOM IMAGE

Members of the Women's Auxiliary Air Force (WAAF) at a remote RAF fighter station in Scotland decided to put on their own Christmas show in December 1943. Here they are seen rehearsing for the big performance.

CLOWNING AROUND

Childishness was actively encouraged at Christmas time. Miss Betty Ruthven Smith was a Voluntary Aid Detachment (VAD) nurse at Bath War Hospital and recalled in 1916 how Christmas could sometimes bring out the worst in her patients.

Just as Weaver, Kelly and I were going off duty we looked into Ward 6 and there was a VAD smoking away! Weaver said that she thought that was going a bit too far to smoke in the ward. Then 'she' spoke and we saw that it was one of their boys dressed up. He was very well got up and made a ripping girl, another boy was dressed up as an old doctor with a beard and specs and a white coat and black trousers. These two played the fool in the corridor and walked up and down arm in arm singing 'If you were the only girl in the world'! They were as happy as they could be.

Harcourt Kitchin served as a Royal Marine in HMS *Berwick* during the First World War. Christmas concerts were a regular occurrence on board ships, although the nature of shipboard entertainment meant that the success of such events was largely dependent on sailing conditions.

One trip out that I remember particular well was Christmas 1917, when we struck very bad seas on the way out and we got green sea right through the wardroom galley. And everything, all the fresh food disappeared and we had a Christmas dinner of salt pork and rice, which wasn't very appetising. But the sailors of course had to have their fun on Christmas Day. And this ship, which used to have its guns on the main deck where they were quite useless, had had the guns shifted up onto the upper deck. Well that put another five degrees on the roll, which in any case was round about forty degrees! And this is what she was doing. Well they had to have their concert, so they brought a piano down – somehow – on to the aft deck, lashed it to a stanchion and they got cracking. But unfortunately, the lashing gave way in the middle and the piano took charge and the concert really finished up with the sailors chasing a piano all over the deck!

A group of patients at the 104th British General Hospital in North Africa, 20 December 1945.

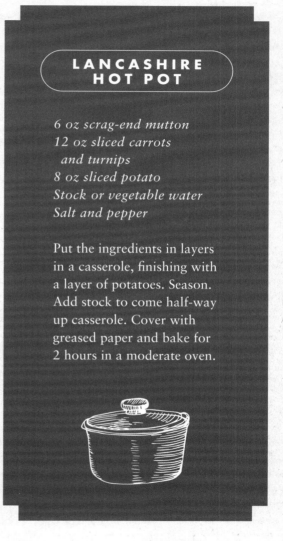

LANCASHIRE HOT POT

6 oz scrag-end mutton
12 oz sliced carrots
  and turnips
8 oz sliced potato
Stock or vegetable water
Salt and pepper

Put the ingredients in layers in a casserole, finishing with a layer of potatoes. Season. Add stock to come half-way up casserole. Cover with greased paper and bake for 2 hours in a moderate oven.

〈

Patients and staff pose in the one of the wards of Bighi Hospital, Malta, decorated for Christmas 1917.

Nurses entertain one of their patients in Kingseat naval hospital, Aberdeenshire, in December 1941.

⌄

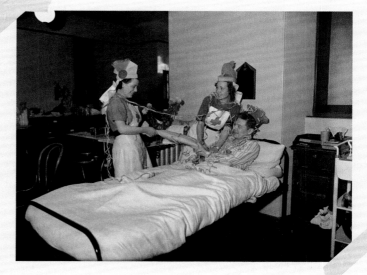

HOMESPUN FUN

Wartime life on the home front usually meant more work for everybody and less time for fun, and so recreational opportunities had to be seized upon when offered. Miss Beatrix Pyne was employed as a Land Girl on a farm in Little Faringdon, Gloucestershire, in 1942. Much of her Christmas Day morning and afternoon had been spent milking, feeding and cleaning out the cows, but Boxing Day evening finally provided an opportunity for some fun.

Joan, Audrey and I went to the Filkins dance in the evening; it was a very villagey, dusty, rowdy affair with plenty of kicks and noise, but we quite enjoyed it. One thing we didn't lack [were] partners, although they were only local bumpkins. I had three coming up at once and chose the tallest. It got very hot and smoky and we were glad to get outside again to cycle back. There's nothing to beat the fresh air, even if it's cold. I should hate to be indoors again now.

Such homespun amusement was epitomised by the forces 'gang show', in which individuals contributed songs, jokes, sketches and other such acts. It was common at the time for many people to have their own well-practiced act to perform at events like this, whether it was a particular piece played on the piano or the recitation of an amusing poem, and Christmas was the perfect opportunity for such repartee. One such performer was Douglas Heathfield-Robinson, serving with the Royal Army Service Corps (RASC) in Holland in 1944.

Christmas Night, Cassel, 1917 by William Orpen.

The concert party group were formed and were given the afternoons off to prepare our acts provided we rehearsed in the evenings, for which we were excused guard duties which in itself was a bonus! In the show Jack played both the piano and the trumpet. We also had an accordionist, a guitarist, a 'Houdini', a fire-eater and a strongman bending iron bars and tearing telephone directories! There were also a couple of singers and, to finish off the programme, a magician. On Christmas night and Boxing night the concert was staged in a small cafe, so we had to have two performances to allow all the Company to see it. The show was a resounding success, both performances lasting two and a half hours. Major Badger then decided that we should do another performance the next night to entertain our Dutch hosts with whom we were billeted, and this was also much appreciated.

<

The Entertainments National Service Association (ENSA) was set up in 1939 to provide entertainment for the British armed forces. They organised concert tours featuring favourite stars of the stage and screen, and Christmas galas were particularly memorable. This particular matinee performance was at Gibraltar on 7 January 1943.

STEAMED DATE PUDDING

*6 oz plain flour and 3 level
  teaspoons baking powder,
  or 6 oz selfraising flour
¼ level teaspoon salt
2–3 oz chopped or
  shredded suet
4 oz dates, chopped
1½ level tablespoons sugar
1 beaten egg (optional)
Approx. ¼ pint milk and
  water to mix*

Sift the flour, baking powder (if used) and salt, add the suet, dates and sugar and mix well. Mix to a soft dropping consistency with the egg and liquid and turn into a greased basin (1½ pint size). Cover with greased paper and steam for 1½ hours. Turn out and serve with a custard or syrup sauce. Serves 4.

This poster advertises a Christmas concert in aid of the Professional Classes War Relief Council. This particular charity sought to identify distress among those from the 'professional classes' and would organise relief and assistance accordingly.

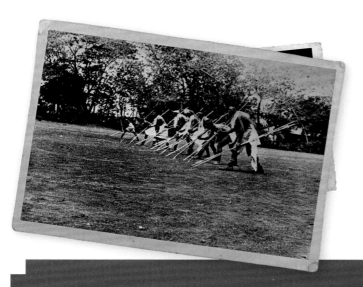

Askari soldiers of northern Rhodesia celebrated Christmas 1942 in Madagascar with feasting, traditional dancing (pictured here) and sports.

WARTIME CHOCOLATE PUDDING

2 cups flour
1 cup grated carrot
1 oz sugar
2 tablespoons golden syrup
1 teaspoon bicarbonate soda
1 teaspoon baking powder
1 heaped tablespoon cocoa
¼ pint milk
2 oz margarine
A little vanilla essence
Salt

Cream the margarine and sugar together and stir in the grated carrot, syrup, fruit and the rest of the dry ingredients. Add milk to mix to a fairly stiff consistency. Put into a greased basin and steam for 2 hours.

ENTERTAINMENT
IN CAPTIVITY

The notion of generating one's own entertainment was particularly important for those in wartime captivity, as prisoners of war and civilian internees were limited in terms of recreational possibilities. Joseph Napier of the South Wales Borderers saw through Christmas 1917 in a prisoner of war camp in Turkey.

Well Christmas of course at home is a tremendous day, one can go out and shop and do all sorts of things. In our case it was, as far as I remember, a very humble affair... We had a sort of dinner party, such as a dinner party was. And we acted this little play, which may have amused them or may not. But I think as far as I remember that was about the only celebration we had at Christmas.

Those in enemy hands during the Second World War were no different. Colonel Harold Sell of the Durham Light Infantry was captured at Gazala in North Africa in June 1942. He ended up in the prisoner of war camp PG 47 at Bari, on the eastern coast of southern Italy, where he and his fellow captives would be forced to use their imagination and initiative to create their own fun.

I have spent some peculiar Christmas celebrations but this bids fair to exceed the lot. The entertainment section announces that we will all be invited to dine at the '21' Club and to witness the cabaret. Guests must pay for admission by rations and parts of Red Cross parcels. We are also bidden to go in fancy dress which is not a hard thing to do in our present state of wardrobe.

Two sailors carry the Christmas tree and holly for seasonal festivities onboard a destroyer flotilla moored in Liverpool, December 1941.

Promptly at 6pm Robby and I present ourselves at the portals of the Club and are received in grand style by a flunkey who passes us on to another so that our arrival can be announced to the assembled company. The Club is tastefully decorated and the tables covered with designed covers made from 'Il Popilo' [a Fascist newspaper]. An orchestra renders 'soft music'. The dinner is a great success, God knows what concoctions we consume but our stomachs are pleasantly tight and a tot of vino adds the rose coloured glasses.

Captivity meant that the prisoners lacked female company, but this did not stop some enterprising and brave individuals from dressing up to impersonate the missing female element. The harsh reality of POW life was forgotten, albeit briefly.

The 'Ladies' add charm to the gathering — possibly the blue painted 25 watt bulbs helped matters — but they arrive in exotic creations to the great slaughter to the Italian bedclothing. 'The Belle of the Ball' has a cigarette holder 10 inches long made from newspaper, gum and a gas cape. Needless to say the floor show went off in a dashing manner with many daring exhibitions of 'native' dancing. The orchestra switched over to 'hot rhythm' and the 'Wizard with the Water' filled glasses and inverted tins. Fairly whipped up the Rhumbas. The Italians gazed at us in awe... The next morning is not so good. Robby and I can hardly bear the sight of each other. The Bungalow is a shambles and the sanitary squad on duty petition for a dispensation from one turn on the roster. The 'Ladies' are a bit off colour too as they are suffering from a rash due to the 'cosmetics' which they make from pencils, distemper scraped from walls and dust. In addition it may be funny to make a fancy dress from an Italian blanket or sheet but the humour disappears when trying to remake the bits for a bed and in our case the damage will require a meeting of the Fascist Grand Council to discuss this damage.

MENS CLOTHING INTO WOMENS

Here are some ways in which a man's unwanted garments can be converted to your own use, if you are quite sure he won't want them again after the war.

A DRESS SUIT

will make you a neat town tailor-made; the tails allow ample length for the jacket.

A PIN-STRIPED LIGHT SUIT

provides ample material for a tailored frock. Have it made with a yoke and perhaps a front panel, letting the stripes run in different directions. This will look very smart.

A TWEED JACKET

could be cut down to your own measurements and you could then wear it with a flannel skirt and a gay pullover.

PLUS-FOURS

will make you an excellent skirt.

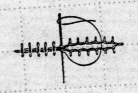

SHARED APPRECIATION

For British prisoner of war Robert Lawrence, imprisoned at Luckenwalde in Germany in 1941, one of the most interesting aspects of the camp's Christmas celebrations was observing how their German captors celebrated the season. By decorating their sparse quarters, the prisoners even managed to impress the normally stern camp commandant.

> He came in and looked round, noting that we had made ourselves an Xmas tree and adorned it with little fancy things, decorated the roof with trimmings, and drawn Christmassy sketches on the window blinds, etc. and in general done everything possible to make our rooms as bright and homely as possible, endeavouring to make the best of our unfortunate circumstances, and he was so struck with it that he could not face all the other rooms, he turned and went straight back to his barracks. It is true to say that there were almost tears in his eyes when he saw the supreme effort we had made, and it had almost the same effect on him as was effected on Scrooge.

In at least this one camp, Christmas had served to bring both captors and captives together in a shared understanding of the celebration.

∧

British troops celebrate a Christmas meal with staff at the free buffet at Euston Station, London, probably on Christmas Day itself 1917.

＞

Men of the Army Film and Photographic Section, attached to the Eighth Army, pictured with Sally the pig shortly before that year's Christmas celebrations during the Second World War. Sally presumably found that year's Christmas dinner particularly disappointing.

Sports and entertainment could be adapted to the local circumstances. Shown here is the camel racing held at Sheikh Othman in Aden during Christmas 1917.

Worship

OVERSEAS SERVICE

Attending church or religious services over Christmas was, for many during war, an essential part of the yuletide celebration. While churches maintained regular services wherever possible for their civilian congregations, troops serving overseas sometimes had more of a challenge to attend religious worship in whatever way their faith expected. The armed forces sought to provide religious support wherever possible for their troops, but this could prove very difficult indeed for those based at the very front line. Such was the lot of Walter Williams of the Army Service Corps who, although posted in a very appropriate location for Christmas 1917, failed to find himself in a particularly festive mood. For him, romantic notions of warm nights under the stars surrounded by the mystery of the Holy Land were swiftly dispersed.

I remember the rainy season at Christmas time 1917, it was very wet and a wee bit cold too. And our 1917 Christmas dinner was eaten in a dump near Bethlehem. It was the usual bully beef eaten with a jack knife and a little drop of tea from a dixie made on a primus. And that was our Christmas dinner 1917!

For those posted overseas, a unique opportunity to experience Christmas in a way particular to the locality might present itself. Thomas Haley was part of the China Convoy of the Friends Ambulance Unit during the Second World War. Having arrived in Rangoon on 16 December 1941, he would celebrate Christmas in the Burmese town of Lashio, on the road to China.

Christmas Day! Sun shining and quite

warm. Went to chapel in the morning, it was conducted in seven different languages, Burmese, Shan, Chinese, Karen, English, Indian and Kachin. A most interesting service, the different representatives of the countries took the platform at the front of the chapel and spoke. Behind the platform was the font, a pool some seven feet square in which we saw some people baptised by complete immersion after the service. It was good to see all these different races together, bound by their common feeling and expressing the same sort of thing in prayer and singing, although in different tongues.

PAGE 116

An aircrew officer and a guard on night duty listen to a choir composed of the ground crew of No 122 Wing, singing Christmas carols by a Hawker Tempest aircraft. Vokel airfield in Holland, 23 December 1944.

<

Ratings attending a voluntary Christmas carol service in the chapel on board HMS *Victorious*, which was transmitted by microphone throughout the ship.

A Christmas carol service held on board the destroyer HMS *Stevenstone*, docked in Portsmouth in December 1943.

*Divine Service on Christmas Day: a naval padre with
ratings, marines and airmen* by Anthony Gross, 1941.

CHRISTMAS IN CAPTIVITY 2

Celebrating Christmas in an unfamiliar location away from home was also the lot of the prisoner of war. For those now removed from the fighting such as prisoner Robert Lawrence, life in captivity provided considerable time for men to consider the religious meaning of Christmas and to celebrate the season through church services. His first such Christmas in German captivity was in 1941, at Stalag III-A.

My first Christmas service was a carol service which we held at 8pm on Christmas Eve. Our padre applied to the German authorities for permission to hold a service at midnight, but failed in his attempt, unfortunately. At 6pm the same evening, just prior to the service, I held a choir practice with about 18 fellows who suddenly came to me in great enthusiasm to form a choir in time for this occasion. The next service I attended was on Christmas morning at 7.15am – Holy Communion which, to put it mildly, was delightful. The room in which it was held was very cold and very desolate, but no matter; the morning itself was far from pleasant, especially at that otherwise unearthly hour of 7.15am, but no matter – it was Christmas, and such trivial things as the time, place, climate, surroundings and general conditions were of little importance in sight of such an occasion as this of Christmas Day. The service in its beautiful, quiet, simple form took place in normal fashion, and things here were exactly the same as in a homely country village church in England.

Knowledge that those at home would be attending Christmas worship in a similar way was a strong antidote to loneliness and separation. However, as has already been noted, for many people Christmas was still very much just another day of the war. In fact, although not necessarily deliberate targets for enemy shellfire, religious services held near the front could be dangerous conglomerations of men in one location, as medical orderly Stanley Parker Bird recalled at Gallipoli, back in 1915.

There was a case of a carol service held on Christmas Day in the casualty clearing station, where a stray shell from the Turks disrupted the service. Killed the chaplain and injured a number of the personnel who were engaged in the carol service.

Mass being celebrated in Bourg Leopold church, Belgium, on Christmas Eve 1944. Soldiers make up the congregation during the reading of the service by the Reverend J Coghlan.

This beautifully illustrated poster was made by prisoners of war in Oflag IX-A, Rotenburg, and advertises Christmas and New Year meals in the camp.

HYMNS AND CAROLS

The singing of hymns and carols remains one of the elements of worship most closely associated with Christmas. The modern form of carol singing with which we are most familiar had traditionally been a country pursuit, based on local words and traditions; the new urban British proletariat of the Victorian era embraced such songs as a link to their past. Singing as a form of worship and celebration could evoke a sense of calm even among the noise and chaos of war, bringing a brief respite from the harsh conditions of life at the front, as testified by First World War ambulance driver Alice Remington.

One particular Christmas was a really beautiful starlit night, it was Christmas Eve, and a very big convoy came in, but they weren't badly wounded. They were all very cheerful at the idea of getting into a bed and having Christmas in bed. We started singing; I think it was 'Hark the Herald Angels' or something. Anyhow, they all sang and it was such a very quiet, still night and you could hear them going up and winding up and down this hill, these boys singing their hearts out, Christmas carols. It was really a lovely thing, moon shining, and the stars shining and these boys all singing carols as they went up to the hospital. They were so thankful; they knew they'd get a bath and a clean. It was wonderful. I'll always remember that night.

Similar examples of the calming nature of Christmas carols exist for the Second World War. Major Charles Manning was imprisoned in

Argyle Street prisoner of war camp in Hong Kong, having been captured when the British colony surrendered to the Japanese on Christmas Day 1941. The following year would therefore mark his first Christmas in captivity and such circumstances encouraged particular reflection.

On Christmas night 1942, the anniversary of our imprisonment, the officers and men in this camp, 546 in all, gathered in one of the huts for a carol service. I heard this carol ['Silent Night'], one of the most, if not *the* most, beautiful of all Christmas carols, for the first time. You are to imagine the long wooden hut, dim lights faintly illuminating walls hung with clothes, towels, oddments of washing with tins and bottles on the ledges of the frames. Men crowded together standing or sitting on beds, boxes, logs of firewood or roughly made stools each thinking of loved ones far away, each with a thought to wonder if he will see them again, though not for the world would anyone admit it, and then 500 voices singing to the accompaniment of an accordion, our only instrument. The time, the circumstances, the words and air of the hymn made an impression on me that I cannot convey in words.

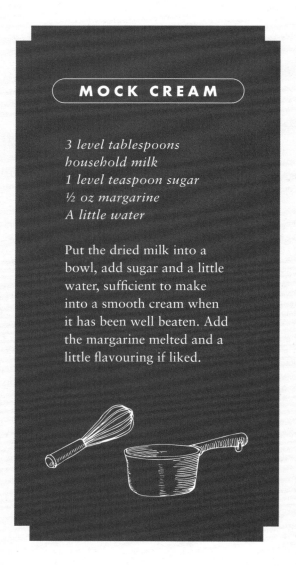

MOCK CREAM

*3 level tablespoons
household milk
1 level teaspoon sugar
½ oz margarine
A little water*

Put the dried milk into a bowl, add sugar and a little water, sufficient to make into a smooth cream when it has been well beaten. Add the margarine melted and a little flavouring if liked.

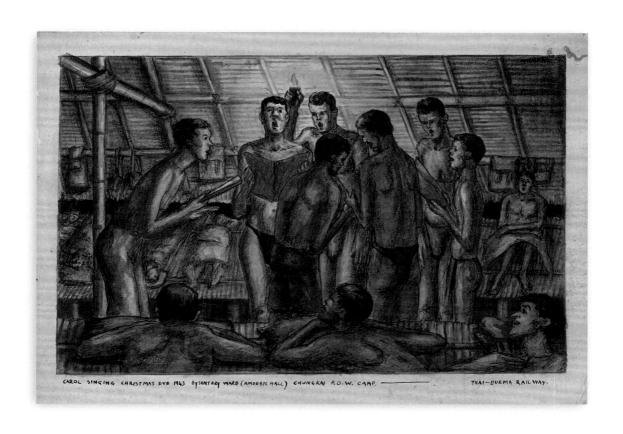

Carol Singing, Christmas Eve 1943
by John George Mennie.

PEACE AND QUIETUDE

Indeed, the peaceful atmosphere spread by Christmas worship could be contagious. Flying Officer R C J Kings found himself in the newly liberated town of Peschichi, in south-eastern Italy, on Christmas Eve of 1944. Midnight mass at the local Catholic Church was about to begin.

The people waited and were quiet. The Church was silent. A little parlour clock hanging on the wall whirred and struck the hour. Twelve silver notes trembled across the white church... it was Christmas Day. There was too much to think of at that moment. I merely stood and stared, quiet and at peace. I thought, all over the world we are standing in our churches, greeting the Child, praying for peace, hushed and seeming humble. And tomorrow? Tomorrow we'll be at it again — all of us — hating, lying, killing... proud and boasting, unquiet, unhappy, with the Child gone out of our souls. Five nuns sang 'Adeste Fidelis'... the beauty of the sound seared my mind. Their little boyish voices were so quiet and as serene as their faces. Voices perfectly trained and perfectly used, as if they caressed something they loved. I wanted to reach out and grasp the music, the instant, the exaltation to keep forever. Silently I cried to them to stop, it seemed more than I could bear. Sentimental? I wouldn't deny it. But the beauty of it I shall remember with a pang to my dying day.

*

A greetings card
specially designed
for the Mediterranean
Expeditionary Force
during the Second
World War.

*Christmas Eve,
Bethlehem: Franciscan
monks ringing the bells
at midnight in the Church
of the Nativity* by James
McBey, 1917

CHRISTMAS · 1940

< This greetings card from early on during the Second World War is already using religious imagery to portray the war as a crusade.

> Just as individual units and formations printed their own greetings cards, hospitals supplied cards to their patients and the relatives of men in their care. This example originates from Horton (County of London) War Hospital in Epsom, Surrey, 1916.

> This 12th Division Christmas card from 1917 reinforces the link between home and the front. Yesterday's farmer is today's soldier.

> This greetings card, designed for the Indian Red Cross in 1944, uses Christmas imagery which would have been appropriate for those serving in the Middle East.

< A Christmas example of a V-mail message, popular among American troops serving overseas during the Second World War. In a similar way to the earlier British 'airgraph' system, a hand-written message would be photographed at source and then transferred via microfilm to be developed and printed back at the home base.

Flying Officer Kings recognised that Christmas could effectively invoke change, bringing peace and goodwill to others during war, albeit on a temporary basis until the fighting resumed. Perhaps it is this aspect which is most important about the celebration of Christmas during wartime; a moment of harmony and normality reminding us of what life could or should be like, before the harsh reality of everyday existence resumes. War and conflict work against many of the notions that Christmas holds most dear, yet our annual celebration of Christmastime serves to remind us of the everlasting possibility of peace.

This attractive card manages to portray a suitably Christmas-like image despite being based on military hardware!

SCRAP BREAD PUDDING

½ pint custard
4 oz stale bread soaked in cold water and squeezed thoroughly
4 teaspoons sugar
Few sultanas

Put the soaked bread into a greased dish and cover with the custard, fruit and sugar. Put a little fat on top if possible and bake in a moderate oven for about 25 minutes.

Shipwrights in HMS *Dunluce Castle* constructed this nativity model for display in the ship's chapel, Christmas 1942.

IMAGE LIST

INTRODUCTION
Art.IWM PST 16433, Art.IWM PST 15609, D 23013,
Art.IWM ART LD 800, Documents.4817/A,
Documents.4817/B

CHAPTER ONE
Art.IWM PST 17277, Q 50721, Q 64568, Art.IWM ART 3137,
HU 55949, TR 2567, EPH 2039, EPH 2041, Q 1631,
Art.IWM PST 15124, Art.IWM PST 3627, Art.IWM PST 10134,
K 62857-1, K 04/992, K 03/470, K 74170, K 04/543

CHAPTER TWO
A 13308, A 13323, A 13389, A 21222, D 23296, FRE 7068,
Art.IWM PST 10776, Q 54267, Q 8354, E 6087, E 10182,
K 02/1922, K 02/2080, K 26566

CHAPTER THREE
Art.IWM PST 1797, D 23619, D 5699, K 87/324,
Art.IWM ART LD 5137, Art.IWM ART 15989 4, EPH 3663,
EPH 4695, HU 20276, NA 20672, A 19530,
Art.IWM PST 10970, K 47441,

CHAPTER FOUR
A 2258, Q 1627, Art.IWM ART 3062, Art.IWM PST 10804,
TR 2569, HU 42353, B 13013, Art.IWM ART LD 2281,
Q 26536, Q 108312, Art.IWM PST 10793, Art.IWM PST 7611,
Q 6401, K 35382-6, K 70232-1

CHAPTER FIVE
A 6485, Art.IWM PST 1074, A 13434, A 13436, A 13552,
A 14184, Art.IWM ART 2989, A 20920, CH 11829,
HU 129303, Q 13070, Q 54274, K 4336, Q 112597,
NA 26559, NA 7819

CHAPTER SIX
Art.IWM ART 17877_43, A 20954, A 13520, A 6742,
Art.IWM ART 1531, B 13098, Art.IWM ART LD 2097, CL 1736,
D 23292, K 93/571-3, K 02/1402, K 04/1344, K 93/571-1,
K 92/2500, K 93/2045, K 49232, Documents.7317
iStock images courtesy of martijnmulder, tmietty,
Zakharova_Natalia, jessicahyde, tomograf, AnnaBliokh
and billnoll

SOURCES

IWM DOCUMENTS

Documents.1684
© the estate of W B P Spencer

Documents.25158

Documents.7818

Documents.13115

Documents.16699

Documents.26162

Documents.11882

Documents.3828

Documents.13128

Documents.7843

Documents.9784
© the estate of J Coles

Documents.1807
© the estate of Viola Bawtree

Documents.19954

Documents.2926

Documents.17429

Documents.16214

Documents.12929

Documents.15374

Documents.13569
© the estate of G L Ruthven Smith

Documents.12130

Documents.888

Documents.17121

Documents.19279

Documents.17377

Documents.4415

IWM SOUND ARCHIVE

IWM Sound 11440, reel 8

IWM Sound 8781, reel 4

IWM Sound 732, reel 6

IWM Sound 330, reel 9

IWM Sound 9884, reel 13

IWM Sound 8328, reel 3

IWM Sound 8868, reel 5

IWM Sound 10600, reel 4

IWM Sound 9790, reel 7

IWM Sound 4147, reel 1

IWM Sound 7499, reel 12

IWM Sound 9754, reel 3

IWM Sound 7375, reel 5

IWM Sound 511, reel 5

ALL RECIPES TAKEN FROM VICTORY IN THE KITCHEN, FIRST
PUBLISHED BY IWM IN 2016.
ALL INFORMATION ON PAGES 53, 79 AND 111 TAKEN FROM
MAKE DO AND MEND, FIRST PUBLISHED BY IWM IN 2007.